Dog Applause

Let's Hear It For

Beagles

Written by

Piper Welsh

Rourke
Educational Media

rourkeeducationalmedia.com

*Scan for Related Titles
and Teacher Resources*

www.rourkeeducationalmedia.com

PHOTO CREDITS: Cover, © Ksenia Krylova; Page 4: © Andrea Krause; Page 5, 17: © Christopher Howey; Page 6: © Marina Maslennikova (Borzoi), © Jagodka (Pharaoh Hound), © Yuri Arcurs (Basset Hound); Page 7: © lendry; Page 8: © Sigurdur William Brynjarsson; Page 9, 10: © Lynn Stone; Page 11: © Ralph Oechsle; Page 12: © Duncan Walker; Page 13: © Lynn Stone; Page 14: © verity johnson; Page 15: © Lisa F. Young; Page 16: © drbimages; Page 18: © Lorpic99; Page 19: © Davide Ciccarello; Page 21: © iztok noc; Page 22: © Fesus Robert

Edited by: Precious McKenzie

Cover design by: Renee Brady
Interior design by: Ashley Morgan

Library of Congress PCN Data

Welsh, Piper.
  Let's Hear It For Beagles / Piper Welsh.
    p. cm. -- (Dog Applause)
  Includes index.
  ISBN 978-1-62169-8715 (hardcover)
  ISBN 978-1-62169-7664 softcover)
  ISBN 978-1-62169-9729 (e-Book)
Library of Congress Control Number: 2013936482

Also Available as:
ROURKE'S
e-Books

Rourke Educational Media
Printed in the United States of America,
North Mankato, Minnesota

Rourke
Educational Media

rourkeeducationalmedia.com

customerservice@rourkeeducationalmedia.com • PO Box 643328 Vero Beach, Florida 32964

Table of Contents

Beagle's happy-go-lucky personality makes them a popular family pet.

Beagles

The Beagle is a good-natured little dog with a big voice. The Beagle may have come from an old French word that meant open throat. It may also have come from an old English word that meant small. In either case, the Beagle seems to have been well named.

Beagle Facts

Weight:	18-30 pounds (8-14 kilograms)
Height:	12-15 inches (30-38 centimeters)
Country of Origin:	England
Life Span:	12-15 years

Beagles are one of the **breeds** in the hound group. The Beagle looks like a miniature version of the Foxhound and **Harrier**.

Borzoi

Pharaoh Hound

Basset Hound

Several other breeds are part of the hound group.

Not only are Beagles good at sniffing out other animals, they also can be trained as detection dogs to sniff out things such as drugs.

Beagles are often called **scenthounds** because of their keen sense of smell. Hunters train Beagles to log onto a rabbit's scent. A trained Beagle will **flush** rabbits for the hunter. As the rabbit runs, the hunter can shoot at it.

Look at Me!

A Beagle has large, round, floppy ears and a square **muzzle**. It has a short-haired coat. The coat is usually a mix of white, tan, and black. A Beagle's tail is long and curves up slightly.

Beagles are sometimes confused with Basset Hounds. Bassets are about the same height. The stout, short-legged Bassets, however, may weigh twice as much as a Beagle!

The square muzzle of the Beagle gives it a distinguished, intelligent look.

The long ears and short legs of the Basset are quite different from the Beagle.

The Beagle's ability to sniff out other animals makes it a perfect hunting companion.

History of the Beagle

Hounds have been around for hundreds of years in different sizes and shapes. Hounds are dogs that were developed to chase and catch mammals. Some hunt mostly from sight, like Greyhounds. Others, like the Beagle and Foxhound, hunt by scent.

Because Greyhounds can run very fast, they can chase down other mammals while Beagles track when hunting.

The exact roots of the Beagle are impossible to know. Beagle type dogs have been known for more than 2,000 years. It is likely that the modern Beagle has **ancestors** from Italy and France in Europe and certainly England in the United Kingdom. One of those ancestors may have been the Harrier. Harriers date back at least 800 years in England.

Harriers are thought to be an ancestor of the modern Beagle.

A Beagle is a keen hunter with great insincts.

Early dog **breeders** wanted a small hunting hound that they could follow on foot. They also wanted a hunting dog they could actually pick up and carry in a pocket. The result was the Beagle.

Beagles of old came in many sizes. Some were just 9 inches (23 centimeters) tall. The modern Beagle was developed in the mid-1800s in England.

The American Kennel Club (AKC) recognizes two varieties of Beagles. One variety has a maximum height of 13 inches (33 centimeters) at the shoulders. Beagles of the larger variety can be up to 15 inches (38.5 centimeters) tall.

The two recognized varieties of Beagles are very similar except for their height difference.

Beagles are always ready to please their owners with love and affection.

A treat is a nice way to show a Beagle you appreciate his gentle personality.

A Popular Breed

Most Beagles are not trained hunters. Beagles are popular for other reasons. One of them is the Beagle's loving personality. Another is that a Beagle is about the size of a loaf of bread. Homes that can't hold a big hound can hold a Beagle.

By 2012, the AKC listed the Beagle as the fourth most popular breed in the United States.

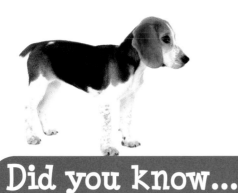

Did you know...

Charlie Brown's pet dog, Snoopy, from the Peanuts comic strip was a Beagle.

A Loyal Companion

Beagles love the companionship of both humans and other dogs. Left alone, a Beagle may bark and howl.

The Beagle's temperament allows it to get along with other canine companions.

A playful Beagle will always find something to bring back to its owner.

Beagles are at their best when they can divide time between the home and the outdoors. Indoors, Beagles are calm but playful.

Outdoors, Beagles love to explore. All dogs live in a world of smells. But the little Beagle is more a slave to its snout than many breeds. Nose to the ground, a Beagle will busily search for new scents. Sometimes the scent leads a Beagle to run off. Even trained Beagles can be stubborn when they're on the trail of a fresh scent.

Some Beagle breeders enter their best dogs in dog shows where they compete with other dogs from around the country. Other Beagle owners enter their dogs in field trials. Field trials test a dog's ability to follow commands for outdoor tasks.

Police departments are now using Beagles as drug dogs. Beagles are able to sniff out illegal drugs hidden in luggage and containers. They are valuable members of law inforcement.

Beagles who compete in field trials do well because of their ability to follow commands easily.

Doggie Advice

Puppies are cute and cuddly, but buying one should never be done without serious thought. Choosing the right breed of dog requires some homework. And remember that a dog will require more than love and great patience. It will require food, exercise, grooming, a warm, safe place to live, and medical care.

A dog can be your best friend, but you need to be its best friend, too. For more information about buying and owning a dog, contact the American Kennel Club at: *www.akc.org/index.cfm* or the Canadian Kennel Club at *www.ckc.ca*.

Glossary

ancestors (AN-ses-tuhrz): those in the past from whom an animal has descended; direct relatives from the past

breeds (BREEDZ): particular kinds of domestic animals within a larger group, such as the Beagle breed within the dog group

breeders (BREE-duhrz): people who raise animals, such as dogs, and carefully choose the mothers and fathers for more dogs

flush (FLUSH): to chase or frighten an animal out of its hiding place

Harrier (HAH-ree-ur): an old, long-legged breed of English hound

muzzle (MUZ-uhl): the nose and jaws of an animal; the snout

scenthounds (SENT-hownz): hounds that use their noses more than their eyes to follow an animal

Index

Websites to Visit

www.akc.org/breeds
www.dogbreedinfo.com/beagle.htm
www.beaglesunlimited.com

Show What You Know

1. Beagles are one of the breeds in which group?
2. What other dog is a Beagle sometimes confused with?
3. A Beagle's coat is usually a mix of what colors?